Original title:
The Roof of My Soul

Copyright © 2025 Creative Arts Management OÜ
All rights reserved.

Author: Christian Leclair
ISBN HARDBACK: 978-1-80587-039-5
ISBN PAPERBACK: 978-1-80587-509-3

Underneath the Stars Within

Underneath the stars, I find my shoes,
They've wandered away with the evening blues.
A cosmic dance upon the ceiling,
Where dreams and laughter spark my healing.

With every twinkle, I lose my socks,
Found nearby, trapped inside some box.
I laugh and sing, my fate's a jest,
In my mind's attic, I'll build a nest.

The Attic of Dreams

In the attic where my luggage lies,
Old suitcases filled with silly sighs.
I search for treasures, find only fluff,
A pillow fort made with giggles and stuff.

A hat from Paris, a sock with stripes,
Mixing mismatched in all types of rites.
Here in my world, nothing's quite right,
But oh how it twinkles in the moonlight.

Celestial Covering

Under a blanket of shimmering dreams,
My thoughts are giggling, bursting at seams.
Stars throw pillows and make silly faces,
Chasing the dust in these mystic places.

A nebula blanket of laughter and cheer,
Whispering secrets that only I hear.
With every snort, I float past the moon,
In a spaceship built from a plastic spoon.

Vault of Hidden Hopes

In the vault of hopes where quirks reside,
An inflatable llama is my joyride.
It giggles with glee as I float in air,
Sharing my secrets, it doesn't care.

There's a treasure map drawn with crayon bright,
Leading to goldfish and laughter at night.
In the party of wishes, we dance and sway,
With interesting friends—who needs ballet?

Reflections on High

Up above, I look and stare,
Pigeons gossip without a care.
My thoughts drift like clouds afloat,
On the sill of my old coat.

Mirrors cringing from my grin,
Laughing at the chaos within.
A squirrel mocks my existential dread,
As I ponder my snack instead.

A Dome of Dreamcatchers

Caught in webs of silly schemes,
Where daylight dances, nothing seems.
Dreamcatchers filter all my woes,
But still, it looks like my nose grows.

Bouncing thoughts on springy strings,
I giggle at the joy it brings.
Like a jester's cap, bright and fun,
I'm the king of my own pun.

Sails of Solitude

My ship sails high on breezy thoughts,
With squirrels to run the jolly knots.
I captain these waves with puns galore,
While laughter echoes on my shore.

A sea of socks, mismatched and free,
In solitude, I find glee.
Joining seagulls' silly squawks,
As they gossip on the docks.

Inner Sanctum of Serenity

In my chamber, chuckles ring,
Where inner peace wears a silly wing.
A cat naps while I caffeinate,
And my worries play hopscotch on a plate.

With cushions piled in laughter's grace,
Every misstep finds its place.
I invite the joy and let it spin,
The dance of calm begins within.

Heights of Forgotten Whispers

In corners made of cotton fluff,
I hide my hopes, they seem too tough.
A squirrel once claimed my morning toast,
While I just sat, a weary ghost.

The ceiling fan's my trusted friend,
It spins my thoughts, they twist and bend.
An upside-down world in a dreary room,
Where socks play dance, defying gloom.

I plan to fly on paper wings,
But gravity, oh, what cruel things!
My dreams just dangle from the light,
Like moths who never learned to fight.

Yet laughter lingers, stout and bold,
In this retreat where tales unfold.
The whispers here, they giggle and tease,
As I sip my tea, unbothered, at ease.

The Limber Sky Within

A circus lives up in my head,
With acrobats who leap from bed.
The thoughts tumble like a carefree clown,
Bouncing high before they fall down.

Juggling dreams with a twist of fate,
A purple monkey in a strange crate.
He winks at me, poising for a trick,
But slips and lands on a candlestick.

The ceilings swirl in shades of blue,
Where clouds poke fun at all I do.
They tease my hair, mess it up nice,
Like I forgot to part it with spice.

Each giggle echoes, fills the air,
A wacky tune without a care.
In this kingdom where my mind takes flight,
I'm the jester, smiling with delight.

Shelter of Echoing Thoughts

Beneath a hat that's far too small,
My thoughts bounce off and hit the wall.
They echo back, a silly crew,
Singing songs I never knew.

A cat is plotting world domination,
While I scheme for a snack vacation.
The fridge is bare, oh what a shame,
But my mind's a chef, igniting flame.

With kitchen pots that dance and sing,
And ingredients that jump like spring.
I make a feast of whispers grand,
As imaginary friends lend a hand.

In this abode where giggles reign,
I find the joy in all the mundane.
Each thought a blessing, wrapped in cheer,
I laugh aloud, for magic is near.

Canopy of Silent Whispers

Up in the rafters, secrets play,
They turn cartwheels, they laugh and sway.
A gossip vine spins tales so tall,
Of hats that clogged the bathroom hall.

Under the beams, a shadow pranced,
In polka dots, he twirled and danced.
His antics made the dust bunnies sigh,
They formed a band of songs to try.

The echo of laughter paints the walls,
While the moon peeks in and gently calls.
With shadows flapping, I hold my breath,
In this crazy space that mocks good sense.

So as the night stretches wide and weird,
I toast to humor, unafraid, unfeared.
Under the canopy, swirling bright,
I find my joy, my heart takes flight.

Dome of Lingering Shadows

Underneath a big, round hat,
I ponder deep, a well-fed cat.
The shadows dance and wiggle about,
While I pretend to snooze, no doubt.

A squirrel may think it's clever news,
But I'll outwit him with my snooze.
The sun is bright, the day is old,
Yet here I sit, so well controlled.

A dance of light, a game of chance,
The ants parade in tiny pants.
Oh, life is grand, or so they say,
As I bask in my own cafe.

With giggles held in playful glee,
The shadows whisper secrets to me.
I chuckle soft, then start to think,
My dome of dreams, not just a wink!

Shield of My Inner Peace

In my fortress made of cheese,
I find a place where I can breathe.
The walls are thick with laughter's sound,
And jokes like glue keep joy unbound.

Each step I take on peanut floors,
Leads to rooms where joy just soars.
Procrastination? Oh, that's my game,
In my shield, it's all the same!

A pillow fight with pillows round,
Is the peace that I have found.
With giggles plucked from dreamland's strings,
I shield myself with silly things.

My armor made of whimsy bright,
Is a sight that brings delight.
Nestled tight in this embrace,
I occupy my happy space!

The Asylum of Unspoken Words

In a room where whispers play,
The voices have their own ballet.
With wobbly chairs and thoughts that tease,
I sit with coffee, feeling at ease.

A turtle's come to seek my thoughts,
He says they're tangled in silly knots.
I nod and grin, but never share,
The asylum's secrets seep through the air.

The walls are scribbled with deep ideas,
Yet all we do is laugh and cheer.
The unspoken flows like fizzy drinks,
While everyone nods, but no one thinks.

So here we dwell, a merry crew,
No serious talk, just giggles accrue.
In this quirky space, it's quite absurd,
Where silence dances; it's never heard.

Lantern of Inner Cosmos

With a lantern lit in my own head,
I wander through thoughts, where few have tread.
Cosmic giggles, they light the way,
As I trip over what I meant to say.

A comet zooms past my funny bone,
And planets tickle, oh what a tone!
With every chuckle, the stars react,
In my universe, there's no one exact.

Nebulas bloom with silly sights,
And I dance among the starry lights.
In this galaxy, fun's always near,
Where laughter's the music that we all hear.

So let the lantern shine so bright,
Creating wonders of sheer delight.
As I float through space with glee unscrolled,
In my inner cosmos, stories unfold!

Hearth of Forgotten Wishes

In the corner, old dreams nap,
Gathering dust, like a cozy cap.
They whisper tales, a ticklish tease,
Of pizza nights and late-night wheeze.

Forgotten wishes, they stir and sigh,
Pining for cookies, oh me, oh my!
A marshmallow roast, an old campfire,
In this warm nook, dreams never tire.

Archway of Reflection

Beneath this arch, I play a game,
Mirror, mirror, who's to blame?
The pizza stains or the window light?
Or the funny hat that gives me fright?

I see a chap with a turtleneck,
Dancing clumsily, what the heck!
I laugh and snort, oh what a sight,
Reflecting joy, oh what delight!

Skylight of Rapturous Silence

Through this skylight, clouds float by,
Whispering secrets, oh my, oh my!
They tickle my thoughts with funny schemes,
While I ponder life and its quirky themes.

Cats on roofs and dogs that sing,
The hilarity of an unseen fling.
In silence that's bursting with laughter's glow,
The sky's my stage, enjoy the show!

The Overhang of Illumination

Under this overhang, I dream and grin,
Cousin Lou's stories, where do I begin?
With gnome-like hats and dancing toes,
And his pet parrot who frequently doze.

The light comes dim, but spirits high,
We share old jokes that never die.
An overhang of giggles, such a treat,
In this comedy, life's bittersweet.

Stars Beneath My Skin

I wear my secrets like a coat,
With twinkling dreams that softly float.
Each laugh a comet, bright and loud,
I dance beneath my own star crowd.

My skin's a map of silly tales,
Of mishaps, giggles, and fluffy sails.
If you poke me, giggles might emerge,
Like bubbles bursting from the urge.

In every freckle, stories hide,
Of cookie crumbs and dreams that ride.
Under the light, my patterns shine,
With every poke, a fun design.

So if you see me chuckle loud,
It's just my stars breaking through the cloud.
With jokes and jests stitched in my seams,
I'm a constellation of silly dreams.

A Shield for the Heart's Journey

I carry a shield made out of laughs,
It's dented from my silly gaffes.
Each giggle pops a worry's bubble,
Turned every stumble into a ruble.

It's painted bright with joy and cheer,
A fortress built with laughter near.
When the road gets bumpy and rough,
I just smile, say, 'Hey, that's enough!'

With every step, my shield will gleam,
Reflecting all my fun-filled dreams.
A heart that's light can conquer storms,
With humor woven in all forms.

So if my journey starts to bend,
I simply wave my shield, my friend.
With laughter locked inside my heart,
I travel on, not torn apart.

Archways to Tomorrow

I built some arches made of jokes,
Each one a portal for silly folks.
With laughter spilling from every side,
Where even grumps have nowhere to hide.

Tomorrow waits, a dopey face,
With dreams and giggles in every space.
I leap through arches, full of cheer,
Spreading joy as I wander near.

Every arch a tickle, a tick, a tock,
A funny dance on the beat of a clock.
With silly hats and shoes that squeak,
We'll find tomorrow, quick and meek.

So come with me, let's make it bright,
We'll jump through arches, in pure delight.
With humor as our guiding star,
We won't just walk, we'll soar afar!

Celestial Embrace of Existence

In a universe of quirky things,
Where laughter dances, and joy takes wings.
My essence twirls in a silly spin,
With cosmic giggles tucked within.

Embrace the odd, it's quite the sight,
The stars all wink with pure delight.
They sing a tune, a goofy sway,
That brightens up the dullest day.

In every corner, humor glows,
Like comets with their silly shows.
Existence tickles, grins so wide,
With every laugh, we take a ride.

So float with me through cosmic haze,
In this embrace of funny ways.
With every chuckle, we surely know,
The universe laughs, it puts on a show.

Ascending Currents of Thought

Up I go, like a balloon,
Chasing thoughts around the room.
With a giggle and a puff,
I find the air is feeling tough.

Clouds of whimsy swirl around,
On my head, they dance and bound.
Oh, the laughter fills the air,
As I float without a care.

Ticklish breezes tease my mind,
In this flight, more fun I find.
Ideas bounce like rubber balls,
While gravity just laughs and calls.

So here I soar, a silly kite,
In a world of pure delight.
With each thought that takes to wing,
I forget the woes that life can bring.

The Overhead Horizon

Look up high, oh what a show,
Birds in bow ties, dance and flow.
They gossip about the clouds above,
Spreading cheer, a feathered love.

The sky's a canvas painted blue,
With polka-dots and stripes, too.
A parade of whimsy trails the sun,
Juggling rays, oh what fun!

Giggles echo from the stars,
Planets strut in tiny cars.
Comets race and tease the moon,
While I hum a silly tune.

So, I lie beneath this grand display,
Wishing clouds would float my way.
In this circus up so high,
Life is a laugh, let's give it a try!

Skylight of Unseen Paths

Bouncing beams of sunlight dance,
Through the cracks in beams, a chance.
Whimsical shadows play around,
Creating laughter on the ground.

Each ray a pathway unexplored,
Where the pickle men've stored,
Jars of sunshine, jars of giggles,
Spilling bright and ticklish wiggles.

A window to my wildest dreams,
Where nothing's ever as it seems.
Here the silly squirrels conspire,
To spring from sunlight, oh what fire!

So I peek through my own glow,
Finding joy in life's big show.
Paths unseen, yet oh-so-clear,
With each laugh, I draw them near.

A Dome of Inner Radiance

Within my mind, a circus thrives,
With acrobats and juggling drives.
Each thought performs a daring flip,
On bright ideas, I take a trip.

The ringmaster, dressed in bright reds,
Tells tales of silly, wiggly threads.
While clowns with pies plot their schemes,
Waking wonder in my dreams.

Bold stunts fly high, without a net,
Where laughter's plentiful, you bet!
A dance of joy, a swing of cheer,
In this dome, I feel no fear.

So come and join this merry show,
Where joy and jest just overflow.
Within my heart, the fun's not small,
With radiant laughter, I stand tall!

Turret of Timeless Tales

In a tower, whispers float,
Stories dance like a goat.
Old windows creak with cheer,
As legends draw near.

Chandeliers swing and sway,
Dust bunnies roam all day.
Each bookworms' secret plot,
Is tangled, not forgot.

The tales unravel in jest,
With humor, they are dressed.
Gargoyles grin from their perch,
As laughter starts to lurch.

In this turret of delight,
Silly dreams take flight.
So come, let's read aloud,
And tickle every crowd.

The Clouds Above My Heart

Fluffy puffs float so high,
Like marshmallows in the sky.
They giggle with the breeze,
And tease all of the trees.

Raindrops drop like clumsy jokes,
Tickling nose and choking folks.
With splashes, they unite,
For a goofy water fight.

Every storm is just a laugh,
Nature's comical craft.
Thunder rumbles with a grin,
As I dance in the din.

Above my heart, hilarity flies,
In such silly, sunny skies.
So let the clouds all cheer,
And make my worries disappear!

Passage to Peace

Down a hallway filled with shoes,
The chaos leads to golden views.
Laughter echoes, echoing light,
As socks and slippers take flight.

Each step is a funny dance,
Twirling on the chance.
A doorknob winks with flair,
Welcoming without a care.

The walls play jokes in whispers sweet,
Making even frowns retreat.
With every corner, joy is born,
Inviting us to wake at dawn.

This passage holds no strife,
Just giggles in our life.
So skip our way to grace,
With a smile on every face.

Cathedral of Unseen Battles

Within these towering walls,
Chickens squawk and music calls.
Fighting with pillows, oh so sly,
Under the watchful eye.

Candles flicker with a snicker,
As marshmallow swords make us quicker.
Rats in armor run the show,
Where tickles are the way to go.

With echoes of joy and fun,
Each silly skirmish has begun.
No swords or shields, just grins we wield,
In this cathedral, laughter's our shield.

So let's cheer for this grand jest,
Where humor is our quest.
In battles both unseen and bright,
We'd always choose pure delight.

The Shelter of Solitude

In my quiet nook, I find my socks,
They hide from the world, like sneaky rocks.
Under the bed, they giggle and cheer,
Claiming a party no one else is near.

My walls wear posters, of cats in a race,
They judge my snack choices with a snooty face.
Cushions are thrones where I sit and plot,
World domination via popcorn and thought.

Palate of Inner Colors

The crayon box calls, it's a riot of hues,
But I only use brown, like a chocolate muse.
Painting my dreams with a messy old brush,
Creating a masterpiece, but it's all just mush.

Green for my envy when the pizza arrives,
Yellow for laughter when my cat dives.
Blue for those days when my plans go awry,
But even then, I wear a smile oh so spry.

High Ground of Unseen Battles

In my mind's arena, I wage a grand war,
Against missing socks and a squeaky floor.
Duck under table, take cover behind chairs,
Winning a battle, but losing my cares.

Battles of pillows, soft cushions collide,
As I fend off the laundry that's creeping inside.
My helmet? A cap, my trusty disguise,
I wade through the chaos that never complies.

The Horizon of Uncharted Emotions

Today I feel happy, tomorrow a frog,
Jumping through feelings, I'm stuck in a bog.
Each morning's a jump into untested shores,
With giggles and wiggles, and sometimes, roars.

When life gives me lemons, I chuck them away,
Why make a drink when I can just play?
Dancing through chaos, my heart's feeling bold,
With a wink and a nod, let adventure unfold.

Umbrella of Yearning

When raindrops fell with glee,
I danced wildly, so carefree.
My thoughts took flight like a kite,
Chasing clouds with sheer delight.

A puddle splashed right at my feet,
With every leap, a chance to greet.
Under the splash, my worries fade,
In laughter's arms, my dreams parade.

With a tiny hat and silly shoes,
I twirled with joy, who could refuse?
Each raindrop tickled my mind,
In this deluge, freedom I find.

So let it rain, I'll sing and play,
In this downpour, I'll find my way.
An umbrella of dreams overhead,
In soaked delight, with joy I'm fed.

Fortress of Fading Light

In shadows that twist like jokes,
I built a castle from quirky folks.
With laughter bricks and giggle beams,
I fortified it with silly dreams.

The walls are lined with inside jokes,
Even the guards are just some blokes.
With marshmallow cannons and candy troops,
Defending against all grumpy groups.

As twilight whispers with a grin,
The fireflies dance, let the fun begin.
In this fortress where laughter reigns,
Each fading light brings sweet refrains.

When shadows loom, I wave and cheer,
For in this haven, there's nothing to fear.
With jokes so funny, the night is bright,
In my fortress, all is light.

The Garden Above My Heart

Petals giggle in the breeze,
As sunbeams bounce with playful ease.
Here daisies wear their hats askew,
And tulips dance—oh, what a view!

Butterflies play tag, so bold,
On sweet nectar, they bravely hold.
With the laughter of bees in bloom,
The garden sings away my gloom.

I talk to flowers as they sway,
"Have you ever had a silly day?"
They nod their heads and share a glance,
In this laughter-filled floral dance.

So come and join this merry throng,
In this garden, we all belong.
With every giggle that takes flight,
My heart blooms bright, pure delight.

Tapestry of Inner Sky

I stitched a quilt of vibrant dreams,
With threads of laughter and glowing beams.
Each patch tells a joke, a tale,
Woven in whimsy, it'll never pale.

Clouds of cotton float above,
Where every corner whispers love.
Stars giggle like ticklish sprites,
Glistening softly on ridiculous nights.

When I lay beneath this silly dome,
I float away from the world I've known.
With constellations that wink and tease,
The vastness holds my heart at ease.

So in this tapestry of sighs,
Take a good look—oh, what a prize!
For in this sky of tales so spry,
I find true joy, no reason why.

Chamber of Whimsical Echoes

In a room full of giggles and socks,
Laughter dances like playful clocks.
Whispers of jokes float on the breeze,
Funny faces and silly tease.

A tickle fight breaks out on the floor,
As rubber chickens squeak and roar.
Invisible friends join in the game,
Each one crazier, none the same.

Lemonade spills on the paper walls,
While the ceiling sings out funny calls.
A concert of chuckles and snickers tonight,
As shadows leap and take flight.

Here, silliness reigns like a king so bold,
With every twist and turn, laughter's gold.
In this chamber, the wacky dreams thrive,
Where nonsense blooms and spirits arrive.

Shelter of Ascending Wishes

In a hut made of wishes, I find my place,
Giggling starlings with silly grace.
Up, up they flutter, like balloons in flight,
Tickling the moon in the soft, warm night.

Toasters that toast only bread of hope,
Jokes on the walls make reality cope.
Here, fancies unfold with a wink and a nod,
As the wind tells tales that are perfectly odd.

The roof of dreams, made of marshmallow puffs,
Wobbly structures, but never too tough.
Wishes take wing and soar like a kite,
Into the heavens, what a glorious sight!

In this quirky abode of delight and glee,
Every wish sprouted in pure jubilee.
A shelter where smiles and laughter blend,
Each day a new joke, each moment a friend.

The Threshing Floor of My Heart

In a barn where love's laughter sways,
Grains of joy run wild in playful bays.
With scythes of humor, we cut through the dark,
Harvesting giggles, a true funny spark.

Wheat stacks lean like dancers in trance,
As chickens join in a clucking dance.
The hay bales bounce to a jolly beat,
Where each jest trips up, a slippery feat.

Beneath the sun, mirth rises high,
Happiness flutters like birds in the sky.
Fields of chuckles, rolling in hills,
As the heart's threshing floor spills over with thrills.

A dance of flavors in every joke,
As laughter brews warm like sun-drenched smoke.
Here, the rhythm of life plays so sweet,
In this cozy harvest, love fills every beat.

Pinnacle of Private Journeys

On peaks where silliness takes its stand,
A mountain of giggles, not so bland.
With each step upward, more laughs unfold,
As butterflies tickle the tales retold.

I climb with a backpack of wacky schemes,
Carrying dreams and comedic memes.
To explore the roads of nonsense and play,
Where comedy queens and kings hold sway.

The summit sparkles with humor divine,
Where puns grow wild and giggles intertwine.
At this height, the world looks so bright,
With a glorious view of pure delight.

Here, every wrong turn leads to sweet laughs,
As life's wild ride creates the best gaffs.
In this place where humor takes flight,
I journey on, with joy as my light.

Arch of Perpetual Dawn

The sun unfurls its golden arms,
Silly shadows dance with charms.
Roosters crow like honking geese,
In this raucous morning peace.

The laughter spills like morning tea,
A cat does yoga, oh so free.
Birds chirp jokes in awkward tones,
While squirrels build their tiny thrones.

Coffee brews with extra foam,
A rubber duck floats near my home.
The world awakes in mirthful glee,
With every joyful cup of tea.

As daylight breaks with goofy sighs,
I chase my thoughts beneath blue skies.
With every chuckle, life's a fun run,
In this arch of perpetual sun.

The Pagoda of Luminous Thoughts

In a pagoda made of giggles,
My mind dances, shakes, and wiggles.
Ideas bounce like rubber balls,
In twinkling halls with silly walls.

A thought might wear a funny hat,
Pretending to be wise; imagine that!
Wisdom here seems full of cheer,
Like a clown with a bright red sphere.

The candles flicker with a tease,
As whispers float upon the breeze.
I scribble down my wildest dreams,
In lollipop colors, bursting beams.

Each notion hums a jolly tune,
As I sip tea beneath the moon.
In this pagoda, laughter sways,
With bright thoughts dancing through the days.

Camera Obscura of the Heart

With a lens of laughter, I take a peek,
At fuzzy feelings, oh so chic.
Snapshots flash, a clumsy view,
Where heartbeats giggle and love comes true.

A blurry kiss beneath the stars,
Captured quick, like racing cars.
Emotions swirl like pastel paint,
While butterflies wear sneakers quaint.

The shutter clicks, a joyful noise,
As my heart plays with silly toys.
Each frame a moment ripe with cheer,
Where even frowns can disappear.

In this camera, love's a riddle,
Exploring life and all its twiddle.
With snapshots framed in whimsy's art,
The essence shines, a joyful heart.

The Terrace of Beating Dreams

On a terrace where shadows play,
My dreams bounce high like a runaway.
They leap and twirl, like kids at dawn,
Making me giggle before they're gone.

Each thought wears shoes of bright confetti,
Prancing about, oh, aren't they petty?
Some dreams claim to be quite grand,
While others just wave a tiny hand.

Clouds lounge like a lazy cat,
While daydreams sit and converse on that.
A rooftop sparked with playful schemes,
Whispering tales of life's silly beams.

As laughter echoes through the skies,
I gather dreams like butterflies.
In this terrace of jubilant beams,
Life dances sweetly with our dreams.

A Canopy of Dreams

Above my head, a canvas wide,
With rainbow splotches, mismatched stride.
A dance of thoughts, both bright and strange,
As goofy visions skip and change.

Clouds shaped like cats and giant pies,
Floating by in a wobbly guise.
I giggle loud at my whims in flight,
Bouncing ideas that shine so bright.

Beneath this dome, I laugh and prance,
Inviting chance to lead the dance.
The stars wink down, they join my jest,
In this circus of dreams, I'm truly blessed.

So if you peek beneath this shade,
You might just see the joy I've made.
In this silly realm where giggles bloom,
My mind's a carnival, dispelling gloom.

Beneath the Celestial Veil

In strange twilight, where shadows dance,
I find my thoughts in a wobbly trance.
With twinkling lights that laugh and beam,
I'm lost within a whimsical dream.

Stars giggle softly, their light a tease,
They twirl and wiggle like clumsy bees.
The moon, a jester with a cheeky grin,
Invites my worries to jump in the bin.

Comets whizz by, with a honk and a laugh,
As cosmos play games, they start to graph.
I roll on the floor of the galactic show,
Where the ridiculous reigns, and the funny must flow.

So here I lie in this cosmic frame,
With joy as my ship, and laughter my aim.
Beneath this shroud of celestial fun,
The absurdity dances — it's never done!

The Tapestry of Inner Heights

In a tapestry woven with colors bright,
Sit silly thoughts that take to flight.
Like socks on a cat or a fish in a hat,
My mind spins around, oh imagine that!

Each thread a giggle, each stitch a smile,
Crafting my world in a playful style.
Sometimes I wonder, Why do socks flee?
They dream of big adventures, just like me!

With heights that tickle and loops that cheer,
I climb these yarns without any fear.
A trampoline made of thoughts so light,
Launch me to laughter, oh what a sight!

So grab a thread and join my spree,
Let's weave a story, just you and me.
In this funny fabric, where whimsy ignites,
We'll create a masterpiece of inner heights.

Shelter of Silent Whispers

In a nook where secrets like to hide,
Whispers giggle, unable to bide.
They dance around like raindrops on leaves,
Making mischief, like playful thieves.

Tucked in shadows, where silence sings,
I find the humor that stillness brings.
A chuckle muffled, a snicker discreet,
These quirks of quiet, oh how they're sweet!

I sometimes wonder, in hushed delight,
Do whispers wear capes in the dead of night?
Or play tag with shadows, like children at play,
Creating a ruckus in their own funny way?

So cozy up in this shelter I've made,
Where chatter goes muted and jokes parade.
In the sanctuary of silence, take a gander,
You'll find jesters in shadows, oh what a candor!

Refuge of Wandering Thoughts

In the attic of my mind, they dance,
Chasing shadows in a silly prance.
Ideas tumble like socks in a dryer,
Each one sparking a giggle, a fire.

They plot to escape, those rascally thoughts,
Stealing cookies while I'm tied in knots.
But oh, the chaos they leave behind,
A circus show in the fuss of my mind!

Balloons float high, laughter rings loud,
Echoes of folly make me so proud.
With a wink and a grin, they take their leave,
I just hope they don't steal the cleave!

In this refuge of whimsy, I'm free to explore,
A comedy club behind every door.
Wandering thoughts, oh what a delight,
Sprinkling joy from morning to night.

The Pavilion of Hidden Desires

In a garden of dreams, I secretly plot,
To snack on sweet wishes that hit the right spot.
A pavilion stands, my craving's abode,
Where desires swirl like candy in code.

I wish for a pet who can juggle and sing,
And fetch me cool drinks on a hot summer fling.
An elephant that paints would be quite the sight,
While sipping on lemonade, oh what a delight!

My hidden desires dance round like bees,
Buzzing in whispers, no sign of unease.
They poke fun at my plans, saying, 'What if?'
But I laugh it off, embracing the riff.

In this pavilion, imagination runs wild,
With dreams that make even the grumpiest smile.
I sway in a carnival of joy and surprise,
Where every wish sparks laughter that flies.

Canopy of Celestial Insights

Beneath twinkling stars and the moon's soft glow,
Ideas flutter like butterflies in a row.
My thoughts bounce around on this cosmic stage,
Tickling the universe, adding to its page.

With each insight wrapped in glittering hues,
I ponder pizza toppings while wearing my shoes.
What if the stars are just tiny cheese pies?
Sprinkling stardust, oh how time flies!

I'd chat with a comet about jellybean dreams,
Trading wisecracks and cosmic extremes.
Each sparkle a giggle, a wink from above,
The sky is alive, filled with playful love.

Under this canopy, I float with delight,
Juggling my thoughts like a circus in flight.
Celestial insights wrap me in cheer,
In the galaxy's laughter, I disappear.

Keep of Ethereal Dreams

In the keep where wishes flutter like leaves,
Ethereal dreams don capes and reprieves.
They slide down rainbows and munch on the light,
Tickling my fancy, igniting the night.

There's a horse that can hum show tunes with flair,
And a table that dances, with no need for chairs.
In this curious castle of giggles and sighs,
Surreal jesters perform as the moonlight flies.

A dragon that tickles with feathers so bright,
And a clock that spins backward, delighting the night.
Each dream is a prank, a chuckle in disguise,
They leap from the shadows, with mischief in their eyes.

In the keep, where laughter and whimsy abide,
Ethereal dreams take me on a wild ride.
With each twist and turn, I tumble and sway,
In this joyful domain, I wish I could play!

Hollow of the Inner Sanctum

In the hollow of my head, ideas bounce,
Like a kangaroo at a grand old pounce.
Thoughts doing the cha-cha, a silly parade,
Who knew my brain could be this well-played?

Socks on the ceiling, pants on the rug,
My thoughts have started to dance, what a shrug!
Juggling bananas, wearing a hat,
Welcome to Wonderland, cat on a mat!

Fridge magnets spin like dervishes round,
While my inner critic can't help but confound.
A circus of giggles, my mind on a spree,
Just don't ask me where I left my keys!

So here's to the madness, let's celebrate loud,
In the hallways of nonsense, I'm blissfully proud.
With each silly notion and chuckle in tow,
I'll keep tiptoeing through my mental rodeo!

The Summit of Forgotten Roads

At the summit where lost socks giggle and play,
Roads that lead nowhere but bright sunshine's ray.
With each turn I take, a joke plays on repeat,
Mapping the routes of my crazy heartbeat.

A chicken in sunglasses crosses my way,
Quips and quibbles echo the whole livelong day.
Old shoes are my guides in this whimsical trance,
While squirrels debate the meaning of dance.

Down every path, a new giggle awaits,
With signs that point to the silliest states.
I'm map-less and free, so why would I care?
Till I step on a pebble, and hey, there's a bear!

Let laughter be music to lead me along,
Through wild, winding roads, I'll hum a bright song.
So here's to the summit of hilarious cheer,
Where the tales of my travels bring me hearty beer!

Sanctuary of Adventurous Spirits

In a sanctuary that bursts at the seams,
Adventurous spirits weave whimsical dreams.
They fly on the backs of majestic old cats,
With top hats and canes, just look at the spats!

Dancing with clouds in flamboyant delight,
They're juggling marshmallows under moonlight.
Each giggle a spark that lights up the day,
While a potato sings opera in its own way.

A parade of mishaps with laughter to boot,
As frogs in tuxedos engage in a flute.
Oh, the magic that lives in this joyous abyss,
Where each weird little quirk is a reason for bliss!

So let's raise a toast to the spirits that roam,
In the sanctuary where laughter feels like home.
For in every adventure, with joy as the guide,
We find little treasures where silliness hides!

The Umbra of My Inner Universe

In the umbra where shadows play tricks and prance,
My inner universe invites me to dance.
With wiggly stars that laugh and tease,
And comet tails tickling my toes like a breeze.

There's a giraffe in pajamas, reading a book,
While the moon serves snacks, oh, come take a look!
Constellations chatting in riddles and laughs,
As time does a jig on its curvy little paths.

With a flip and a twirl, I orbit the fun,
While marshmallows bounce in a race to the sun.
Bubbles of laughter float high in the air,
As I dive into giggles without any care.

In this universe where silliness reigns,
Every whimsy expands, breaking all chains.
So let's twirl through the shadows, ignite the delight,
For the umbra of joy is a truly grand sight!

Vault of Unwritten Stories

In a vault where dreams collide,
There's a tale of cats who bide.
With hats too big, they dance and twirl,
Chasing after a giant pearl.

A chicken crossed the road to flight,
Cluckin' jokes 'til the morning light.
With feathered friends, they laugh a lot,
Plotting antics on the hot asphalt.

A squirrel wearing shades so bright,
Plans to juggle acorns tonight.
But ends up stuck in a tree so tall,
Yelling, "Help! I'm having a ball!"

In this vault of quirky schemes,
Life's a circus full of dreams.
So grab a drink, let laughter steer,
These stories linger, loud and clear.

The Lookout of Longing

From a lookout perched so high,
I spy a pie in the sky.
With whisks and spoons, the clouds do bake,
Sunny side up, a breakfast flake.

A rumor stirs of fluffy clouds,
They hold a party, drawing crowds.
A rainbow dance, a joyful leap,
Balloons that pop and laughter cheap.

A penguin with a monocle,
Gazes down, feeling quite cynical.
"Why don't we slide instead of waddle?
Let's give our flippers some new throttle!"

Through the longing, smiles await,
In this lookout, we celebrate.
With humor's sparkle bright and keen,
Life's a jest, a joyous scene.

Roofbeams of Radiant Life

Beneath the beams that freely glow,
Lies a secret that few know.
Cats in pajamas, snug and warm,
Dream of cheese, a tasty charm.

A duck that quacks a silly tune,
Hoping for a flight to the moon.
With feathers fluffed and wings spread wide,
He cartoons all while he slides.

A squirrel dons a tiny suit,
Debating if he should join the loot.
"Why not dance 'round the oak so grand?
I'll twirl and whirl, it will be planned!"

In the roofbeams, joy will bloom,
It chases away all doom.
So climb aboard this quirky ride,
In radiant life, let's all abide.

Canopy of Transient Glories

Underneath this leafy shroud,
I hear whispers, oh so loud.
A ghost that tickles with a grin,
Scares the hiccups right from within.

An octopus with a hat so dandy,
Plays in puddles, feeling sandy.
With jokes that splutter from his beak,
He'll have you laughing for a week.

A turtle rides a skateboard fast,
Zooming past the trees amassed.
He shouts, "I'm the king of speed!"
But trips on roots, oh yes indeed.

In this canopy, wonders rise,
Silly stories, none disguise.
Let's bask in glories, quirks galore,
Life's a treasure, we want more!

The Balcony of Soulful Whispers

On a ledge where giggles play,
I spy my thoughts in bright ballet.
The clouds below have socks askew,
They dance with dreams, a silly crew.

Pigeons gossip, what a show,
Cacophony of chit and woe.
A lollipop on breezy air,
My soul's a clown, beyond compare.

A parrot squawks of ice cream fate,
While I sip joy, it's never late.
This balcony, high, a raucous fling,
With whispers bold, my heart does spring.

So here I sit, a jester's throne,
With every laugh, I claim my own.
Between the giggles and the sighs,
A whimsical soul that never lies.

Vantage Point of Hidden Echoes

From cliffs of chuckles, I observe,
A world that spins with every swerve.
The echoes dance, they bubble, pop,
Each giggle's taste, a sugary drop.

A raccoon tells jokes, quite out of line,
While squirrels hold court and drink their wine.
I laugh aloud, a bit absurd,
At every quip I've sometimes heard.

A rubber duck floats by with flair,
Singing ballads into thin air.
In this place, where echoes play,
My spirit twirls, brightens the day.

Up here, I see the world collide,
With humor sprouting, won't abide.
The vantage point, a canvas bright,
Where every laugh brings pure delight.

Pinnacle of Inner Radiance

Atop a peak that sparkles red,
I call my worries, 'go to bed'.
With silly hats and laughter loud,
My heart's a dancer, proud and proud.

The stars above wear goofy grins,
As I parade my witty spins.
Each twinkling light, a friendly face,
In this uplifting, joyous space.

A moonbeam whispers, "What's the joke?"
While shooting stars all dance and poke.
I'm on a rocket of delight,
And humor fuels my nightly flight.

The pinnacle, a cosmic floor,
Where laughter flares forevermore.
In this radiant, cheerful zone,
I find the love I've always known.

Meadow Above the Mind

In a meadow where giggles sprout,
I twirl around, there's no room for doubt.
Butterflies wear shoes of rain,
While daisies sing, 'Come dance again!'

A rabbit jokes about the moon,
While ladybugs hum a timeless tune.
Here, my worries drift away,
In sunshine's glow, I'll always stay.

The grass tickles my soles with glee,
As I hug clouds, oh what a spree!
In this field, the mind can roam,
And every heart learns how to foam.

So let me find a patch of mirth,
Where laughter's worth its weight in worth.
In this meadow, free and wild,
Forever stays the light-hearted child.

The Vista of Veiled Reflections

In the mirror of my mind, I see,
All the jokes that bubble up with glee.
A reflection of laughter dancing bright,
Like socks on a cat in the pale moonlight.

A squirrel with shades, climbing the tree,
Dancing to tunes only he can see.
I chuckle at clouds, they funny clouds,
Dressing up in garbs, of fluffy crowds.

I sip my tea, it spills with a laugh,
My book of jokes turned to a bath.
The fish in the pond, they wink with delight,
As I ponder the bubbles that pop in flight.

So here's to the whimsy, the giggles we share,
In the vista of life, with love and flair.
With every reflection that sparks a smile,
Let's gather our joys, let's linger awhile.

Isle of Tranquil Light

On the isle where the sun always beams,
The shadows do dance, or so it seems.
A crab in a tux, quite dressed for the show,
With a top hat that sways as he moves to and fro.

The waves whisper secrets, a comedian's tale,
As I watch the fish jump, each one a scale.
A flamingo on stilts, struts with great pride,
While seagulls critique from their perch on the side.

I flip a seashell, hear laughter untold,
It giggles and snickers, a treasure of gold.
With sunbeams of joy and sand tickles abound,
Let's dance with the whispers, joyfully sound.

In this isle of light, where silliness reigns,
Every chuckle and snort just loosens the chains.
With whimsy all around, not a care in the air,
Join hands with the sea, let's dance without a care.

The Pavilion of Still Waters

In the pavilion where quiet reigns,
I spot a duck that practices trains.
He waddles and whistles, a seasoned pro,
While frogs form a band with a croaky hello.

The lily pads giggle as I pass them by,
Calling out silly jokes to the clouds in the sky.
The fish tell me tales of their underwater bliss,
While I ponder on life and give laughter a kiss.

In the calmness, I find a sense of cheer,
As the turtles debate the best ways to steer.
Each ripple a chuckle, a wave of delight,
Sparking joy like fireworks lit up at night.

So let's gather our laughter, our whimsical charms,
In the pavilion of water where no one disarms.
For humor's the treasure that everyone needs,
Let it flow like the fountain, where joy's never seeds.

The Attic of Aspirations

Up high in my mind, ideas gather dust,
Like treasures forgotten, in thoughts we trust.
There's a cat in the corner, snoozing away,
Dreaming of fish, while I dream of ballet.

Boxes of wishes, stacked high near the eaves,
Some are all cracked, like old fall leaves.
A ladder to nowhere, I sometimes climb,
And lose my balance, quite comically every time!

The shelves wobble gently, with dreams piled high,
In this goofy place, there's no need to be shy.
I chuckle and giggle at a balloon's flight,
As it bumps the ceiling, what a goofy sight!

Among all the clutter, I find glee and cheer,
For every aspiration, holds laughter near.
With dreams and shenanigans, my heart starts to glow,
In the attic of hopes, I find joy in the flow.

Foundation of Hopeful Visions

In the base of my thoughts, there's concrete delight,
Where plans sprout like weeds, under moon's silver light.
A deck chair for daydreams, slightly askew,
With ice cream wish lists that I always accrue.

Brick by brick, I build with a chuckle and jest,
A tower of giggles, where silliness rests.
The blueprints are scribbles from late night snacks,
With peanut butter murals and ketchup laid tracks.

I invite all my visions to dance and parade,
Through a whimsical hall that I lovingly made.
Every bump in the journey, a story to tell,
In the foundation of hopes, I wish you could dwell.

So come grab your hard hat, let's dig deep with cheer,
We'll find dreams buried under raucous tears.
With a hammer and laughter, we'll build something great,

In the foundation of wishes, we can celebrate!

Celestial Umbra

Beneath a silly moon, where shadows play tricks,
Lies a dance of the stars, as they swap funny kicks.
When comets get shy, they hide 'neath a cloud,
While meteors rush by, looking silly and proud.

The universe chuckles, and so do the moons,
As planets sing songs and bop to odd tunes.
A black hole is laughing, with a snicker and sway,
While galaxies twirl in the most wobbly way.

Oh, the comical chaos, celestial ballet,
As the sun dons sunglasses and shouts, 'Let's play!'
In this fun little cosmos, laughter's the guide,
Floating on stardust, we'll happily glide.

So look up tonight, where the galaxy beams,
And let your heart dance, in the land of sweet dreams.
With a wink from the stars, we find silly delight,
Under the celestial dance, everything feels right.

The Hearth of Hidden Light

At the center of warmth, there's a flicker so bright,
With the crackle of laughter, in the coolness of night.
A kettle is whistling, with bubbles so grand,
While the marshmallows giggle, as they float on the sand.

The logs tell stories, of silliness past,
Of elves who misplace their pointy-toed hats.
In the glow of the fire, my worries recede,
As shadows tell jokes, and merriment breeds.

S'mores start a party, with chocolatey cheer,
Inviting the fruit flies, who buzz around here.
The flame dances, silly, with a flick of its tongue,
Singing sweet harmonies like a song yet unsung.

So gather around, let your heart fill with light,
In the hearth of our chuckles, we'll banish the night.
With joy in the air, let the laughter ignite,
In this cozy abode, everything feels right.

The Shelter of Yearning

In a hat too small, my dreams collide,
Chasing cats, they run, can't let them hide.
A treehouse built from hopes and snacks,
But the raccoons have staged a prank attack.

With a rooftop made of candy canes,
I sing to squirrels through my window panes.
The neighbors think I've lost my flair,
But who can resist a jam with fresh air?

Kites dance on strings of awkward cheer,
I ask the wind, 'Can you lend an ear?'
Balloons are floating like my thoughts,
They pop at laughter, that's how they're caught.

A shelter built with giggles galore,
A place where dreams can leap and soar.
I wave to clouds with a silly grin,
In my happy space, let the fun begin.

Elevation of Echoed Thoughts

In a hat so tall, I think I'll fly,
Step on clouds, just give it a try.
The pigeons laugh, they think I'm bold,
But I'm just a dreamer made of gold.

Elevated thoughts, they float like fluff,
Overthinking life can get pretty tough.
Yet with a snicker and a giggle,
I dance on rooftops, feeling quite the wiggle.

The echo of laughter rings so clear,
It's just my brain, or is that a deer?
I talk to sparrows, they rule the skies,
But I swear they wear little bow ties.

High above the mundane, I find delight,
In cloud-shaped critters playing at night.
While gravity sighs, I'm floating along,
Here in my head, where everything's song.

A Sanctuary of Endless Skies

In a fort made of pillows, my thoughts take flight,
A castle of wishes, all wrapped up tight.
The physics of fun, I've yet to learn,
But I'll launch my dreams with a flick and a turn.

The ceiling fans spin tales of their own,
While my rubber ducks rule over foam.
In a world where socks are often mismatched,
I hear the giggles that dreams have patched.

With stars made of glitter and moonbeams of cheese,
I toss ideas like confetti in the breeze.
Laughter echoes in my cozy domain,
Each thought a balloon, none are ever plain.

A sanctuary where silliness reigns,
You'll find all my thoughts in jumbled trains.
With a wink to the sun and a grin at the moon,
In my sky-high bubble, I'll dance to the tune.

Embracing the Ether Above

Suspended in giggles, I float on a whim,
Caught in the twirl of my own silly spin.
With stars in my pocket and clouds for my hat,
I bounce with delight, like a playful cat.

In the breeze, I send wishes to float,
While butterflies giggle, and bees take note.
They buzz about tales of hysterical heights,
While I pen my thoughts on colorful kites.

With a quirk in my mind and a twist in my heart,
I embrace all the ether, it's truly an art.
In a whimsical waltz with the universe wide,
There's laughter in starlight, a joyous ride.

So let's twirl through the cosmos, hand in hand,
Spinning sweet stories that no one can brand.
In the laughter of echoes, all dreams can abide,
In this silly adventure, we're all on the ride.

Nexus of Eternal Reflections

In the mirror, I stare, what a sight!
A raccoon in a suit, feeling quite bright.
He winks, then he grins, like it's all a game,
"Buy one, get one free—my spirit's the same!"

I juggle my thoughts, each one a balloon,
Floating high, oh so near to the moon.
I trip on a thought, land flat on my back,
Laughing at clouds that just give me a crack.

What if I danced with a talking pine tree?
Twirled in the breeze, no one could see.
It whispers my secrets, so silly and bold,
I'm the life of the party in tales that it told.

My aspirations brew like a steamy cup,
Add sugar and spice, watch my worries erupt.
With each sip, I giggle, like life's a big show,
"More coffee!" I chant, as my dreams overflow!

Promenade across Inner Skies

I stroll through my thoughts, they're quite a parade,
All my ideas, in bright colors displayed.
A dog in a tutu, a cat with a hat,
Step lively, my mind's a whimsical chat!

Clouds prance overhead, they're wearing some shades,
While raindrops get jealous, they keep throwing spades.
"Catch us, if you can!" the sun's rays proclaim,
I giggle and dance, feeling oddly the same.

A balloon tied to dreams, it floats by my side,
We share silly jokes, on this whimsical ride.
With each giggle shared, I soar ever high,
A trampoline bounce in the soft, starlit sky!

The horizons I see, are made of ice cream,
Flavors stacked high, what a wonderful scheme!
I take a big scoop, it's laughter I taste,
With every sweet bite, I'm lost in a haste!

The Fortress of Brewed Aspirations

In a castle of dreams where my laughter resides,
Jesters and muffins share joy on the slides.
A moat filled with tea, with biscuits that float,
I sip and I giggle, while I steer this big boat.

My armor is made from a blanket so warm,
Defending against pranks with the utmost charm.
The dragons are friendly; they bake lovely pies,
Filling the air with their sweet, sugary sighs.

I challenge my fears to a game of charades,
Unicorns cheer as my courage cascades.
A pie in each hand, dodging whips from the cue,
No danger in sight, just a wink and a boo!

With every sip brewed from the cauldron of hope,
My fortress stands firm; it's my way to cope.
Join me on this quest; let's conquer the day,
With laughter and dreams, we'll chase gloom away!

Spire of Unfolding Stories

At the top of my tower, where tales twist and twirl,
I find a lost sock, oh, what a surreal pearl!
It whispers to me of adventures untold,
"Come, join in the fun, let your wild side unfold!"

Each flight of the stairs has a joke on the wall,
A giggle a step, hear the laughter enthrall.
A cat with a sass unmatched in my dreams,
Dances on rainbows, or so it seems!

A library's glow spills stories from shelves,
The characters wink as they dance by themselves.
Ink spills like confetti, a joyous brigade,
Where squiggles and doodles get all unafraid!

I'll craft a new legend with colorful threads,
Of bananas in pajamas that jump across beds.
With every new plot twist, my heart starts to sing,
In this spire of fun, let imagination take wing!

The Landing of Liquid Moments

A cup of tea spills on my lap,
I dance like a fool, what a trap!
Laughter echoes, bright as the sun,
In puddles of joy, we all have fun.

With every sip, the giggles grow,
My cat joins in, stealing the show.
He leaps and winters in a swoon,
While I stumble, twirling like a balloon.

Moments of chaos, sweet and weird,
The clock strikes one, and we're all cheered.
As laughter bubbles in every round,
In this goofy haven, joy is found.

So raise your mugs in playful cheer,
For awkward sips we hold so dear.
Life spills over, we laugh through it,
In liquid moments, let's just admit!

Haven of Whispered Secrets

In corners tight, we share our dreams,
Whispers dance like soft moonbeams.
Secrets slip from lips like jam,
Together we giggle, oh, what a jam!

I tell of crushes, you roll your eyes,
Cackles burst forth, no need for lies.
From hidden spots, our laughter flows,
In this haven, silliness grows.

Socks mismatched, but who really cares?
We fashion outfits from quirky wares.
In whispers shared and joyous shrieks,
We find the fun that friendship seeks.

So let's concoct a tale so wild,
Of unicorns and a dancing child.
In this snug nook of laughter bright,
We cherish secrets all through the night.

The Upper Chamber of Silent Echoes

In a room where quiet lives,
The echoes tease, but laughter gives.
When silence reigns, we make a scene,
With muffled giggles—so serene!

A sneeze erupts like thunder's roar,
We point and laugh, can't take it more.
In silent corners, jokes collide,
We burrow deep, where fun can hide.

The chandelier shakes with every laugh,
We split our sides like a silly half.
Whispers travel, like a soft breeze,
In this chamber, we do as we please.

So let's delight in this quirky sound,
Turn silence up, let joy abound.
These echoes weave a tapestry bright,
In our hidden room, let's dance tonight!

Pinnacle of Serene Visions

On mountaintops where laughter flies,
We balance joy beneath clear skies.
A summit reached, where quirks unfold,
With silly dreams, our tales are told.

Tumbling down in sunlit glee,
We roll like kids, you and me.
At this peak, where giggles soar,
With every tumble, we want more!

Pine trees sway, their branches sway,
As if they laugh at our child's play.
In serene moments, we find our grace,
As funny faces fill this place.

So clap your hands, and stomp your feet,
Join the fun, and feel the beat.
On this pinnacle, we stand so bold,
In visions bright, let laughter unfold!

www.ingramcontent.com/pod-product-compliance
Lightning Source LLC
Chambersburg PA
CBHW060138230426
43661CB00003B/473